James Madison's U.S. Constitution Trivia Challenge

Jonathan Ozanne

ISBN-13: 978-1500531164

ISBN-10: 1500531162

DEDICATION

For Sarah, Josiah, Gideon and Samuel.

In memory of Micah.

CONTENTS

ACKNOWLEDGMENTS

The author is grateful for the encouragement he has received from his family and friends while writing this book.

INTRODUCTION

The U.S Constitution is an important document. It provides a legal framework for the government United States of America. How the Constitution was written, and the government it created distinguishes the United States from other Western democracies. This quiz book offers you a chance to find out how much you know about the United States Constitution.

This book starts out with the Constitutional Convention, what it was, why it was called, and what happened there. The next chapter has questions about the ratification of the Constitution. The next chapter includes some biographical questions about James Madison. He was one of the key figures in the creation of the Constitution. The final section has chapters on the text of the Constitution and its amendments.

This book can be used in a couple of different ways; it can be used to learn about the Constitution and it can be used to play a competitive trivia game.

I hope you have as much fun answering these questions as I had researching and writing them!

Jonathan Ozanne

QUESTIONS

CONSTITUTIONAL CONVENTION

1. What was the original purpose of the Philadelphia Conference of 1787?
   - A. To amend the Articles of Confederation
   - B. To create a new constitution
   - C. To increase the salaries of the members of the Continental Congress

2. What year were the Articles of Confederation proposed?
   - A. 1776
   - B. 1780
   - C. 1787

3. By what year had the Articles of Confederation been adopted by the new states?
   - A. 1781
   - B. 1783
   - C. 1786

4. Who was the primary author of the Articles of Confederation?
   - A. Benjamin Franklin of Pennsylvania
   - B. John Dickinson of Delaware
   - C. Thomas Jefferson of Virginia

5. How many presidents of the United States are there in the government that is provided for by the Articles?
   - A. 0
   - B. 1
   - C. 13

6. Which branch of government was the strongest under the Articles?
   - A. Executive
   - B. Judicial
   - C. Legislative
   - D. They were all equal strength

7. True or False. The failures and shortcomings of the Articles were seen as a threat to national unity?

8. Which of the following was NOT an issue with the Articles of Confederation?
    A. Lack of taxation powers for the central government
    B. It was too difficult to amend the Articles
    C. States' rights were not adequately protected

9. Which Founding Father had an "excused absence" from the Constitutional Convention? (With him present, the Constitution might have turned out very different.)
    A. George Washington of Virginia
    B. Thomas Jefferson of Virginia
    C. Francis "Swamp Fox" Marion of South Carolina

10. The delegation from which state was several weeks late to the Convention?
    A. Georgia
    B. New Hampshire
    C. New York

11. Who presided over the Convention?
    A. Benjamin Franklin of Pennsylvania
    B. George Washington of Virginia
    C. Elbridge Gerry of Massachusetts

12. At the start of the Convention, in late May of 1787, Edmund Randolph, Governor of Virginia, proposed a number of changes to the Articles of Confederation. His ideas are often referred to as the Randolph Plan or the Virginia Plan. According to the Virginia Plan how many Presidents should there be at one time?

    A. 1
    B. 2
    C. 3

13. Whose idea was it to have Presidential vetoes overridden by a two-thirds vote of Congress?

    A. Benjamin Franklin of Pennsylvania
    B. Elbridge Gerry of Massachusetts
    C. Edmund Randolph of Virginia

14. James Madison of Virginia is well-known as "Mr. Constitution" or "Father of the Constitution" for his leadership and authorship roles at the Convention; what lesser known founding father made a somewhat unsuccessful claim of co-author?

    A. Thomas Jefferson of Virginia
    B. Nathaniel Gorham of Massachusetts
    C. Charles Pinckney of South Carolina

15. During the convention, William Paterson of New Jersey introduced a plan favored by the smaller states. His ideas are known as the Paterson Plan or the New Jersey Plan. With what was the New Jersey Plan primarily concerned?
    A. Duties and excise fees
    B. The number of Senators
    C. Dividing the states into 13 equal-sized states

16. Votes at the Convention were generally by state with each state getting one vote. How the state decided to vote on a particular issue was determined by a vote amongst the members of each state delegation. If the delegation could not agree or had a tied vote, the state lost its vote on that particular ballot. What delegation in particular was plagued with divided members and so forfeited the most votes?
    A. Georgia
    B. New York
    C. Virginia

17. What order did the states vote in during the Convention?
    A. Alphabetical order (Connecticut first)
    B. North to south (New Hampshire first)
    C. No particular order

18. Which delegate from Connecticut proved adept at brokering compromises on big disputes that threatened to derail the Convention?
    A. Elbridge Gerry of Massachusetts
    B. Roger Sherman of Connecticut
    C. William Randolph of Virginia

19. Who was chair of the Style Committee and helped reduce the number of articles in the Constitution from 23 to 7 by careful editing?
    A. Nathaniel Gorham of Massachusetts
    B. Elbridge Gerry of Massachusetts
    C. Gouverneur Morris of Massachusetts

20. One of the hotly debated issues at the Convention was where the capitol should be located. At the time of the Convention where was the capitol of the United States located?

    A. Boston

    B. New York City

    C. Philadelphia

21. Which state did not send any delegates to the Convention?

    A. Virginia

    B. Georgia

    C. Rhode Island

22. Why did that state not send any delegates to the Convention?

    A. The Convention was held in secret and that state was not invited

    B. That state was happy with the status quo under the Articles and saw no need to amend them let alone replace them

    C. The legislature of that state was gridlocked and could not choose which among them should have the honor of attending and the Convention ended before the gridlock

23. What was the practical effect of that state not sending any delegates to the Convention?
    A. There was no practical effect
    B. The state received fewer senators than the other states
    C. The state was ineligible for the first presidential election

24. Was an extensive public record of the Convention kept?
    A. Yes
    B. No

25. When did the Convention meet?
    A. Late spring and summer of 1786
    B. Late spring and summer of 1787
    C. Late spring and summer of 1788

RATIFICATION

26. What was the deadline for ratification?
     A. 1 year
     B. 2 years
     C. No deadline

27. Generally how long did state ratifying conventions last?
     A. About a week
     B. About two months
     C. About four months

28. What are the Federalist Papers?
     A. An early equivalent of the Pentagon Papers
     B. Anonymous editorials in support of the new Constitution that appeared in newspapers
     C. The record of the ratification voting in each state

29. Who authored the most Federalist Papers?
     A. Thomas Jefferson of Virginia
     B. James Madison of Virginia
     C. Alexander Hamilton of New York

30. Who authored only a few Federalist Papers?
     A. John Jay of New York
     B. George Clinton of New York
     C. Thomas Jefferson of Virginia

31. Which state was the first to ratify the Constitution?
     A. Delaware
     B. North Carolina
     C. Pennsylvania

32. Which state was the 9th and deciding state to ratify the Constitution (beating the 10th state by only four days)?
     A. New Hampshire
     B. Rhode Island
     C. Virginia

33. Which state was the last to ratify and did so too late to be able to participate in the presidential election of 1789?
     A. Virginia
     B. Rhode Island
     C. New Hampshire

34. What were opponents of ratification know as?
    A. Federalists
    B. Copperheads
    C. Antifederalists

35. How many states did not ratify the Constitution on the first attempt?
    A. 0
    B. 3
    C. 5

36. How many states had ratified by January 3, 1788?
    A. 0
    B. 2
    C. 4

37. Was the Connecticut ratifying convention acrimonious or harmonious?
    A. Acrimonious
    B. Harmonious

38. How many days was the Constitution debated in Georgia?
    A. 1 day
    B. 11 days
    C. 111 days

39. Where did the ratification convention take place in New Jersey?
   A. A church
   B. A tavern
   C. A county courthouse

40. In what city was the New York convention held?
   A. Albany
   B. Buffalo
   C. Poughkeepsie

41. Where did the North Carolina convention take place?
   A. A barn
   B. A church
   C. A tavern

42. What aided ratification of the Constitution in South Carolina?
   A. Persuasion by the federalists, including several brilliant speeches
   B. Endorsement of the Constitution by Revolutionary War hero Francis "Swamp Fox" Marion
   C. Regions of the state where support for the Constitution was weakest were underrepresented at the Convention

43. What famous general sent a letter to a friend in Massachusetts endorsing the Constitution?
    A. George Washington of Virginia
    B. Israel Putnam of Massachusetts
    C. Nathanael Greene of Rhode Island

44. True or False? Ratification in Massachusetts was critical to the success of the Constitution?

45. True or False? Pennsylvania had a rather acrimonious convention and the bad feelings about that convention spilled over into other states?

46. Which answer best describes the Maryland convention?
    A. A close vote with both sides satisfied at the outcome
    B. A lopsided vote with both sides satisfied at the outcome
    C. A lopsided vote with the losers unhappy at the outcome

47. Which of the following was one of the largest and most frequently occurring objection to the Constitution?
    A. Lack of a Bill of Rights
    B. Term limits for each of the branches of government
    C. Increased role of the federal government in regulating commerce

48. Which state was the first state to fail to ratify the Constitution at a convention?
    A. New Hampshire
    B. Rhode Island
    C. Virginia

49. When did preparations begin to hold the first elections under the new Constitution?
    A. Right after the Convention had adjourned because Congress was confident in a speedy ratification by the states
    B. After Congress had certified the results that nine states had ratified the Constitution
    C. After all thirteen states had ratified the Constitution

JAMES MADISON

50. James Madison is most famous for his considerable involvement with the drafting and design of what founding document?
    - A. The Declaration of Independence
    - B. The Articles of Confederation
    - C. The Constitution

51. How tall was James Madison?
    - A. He was one of the shortest presidents
    - B. He was one of the tallest presidents

52. James Madison was the first president to wear what article of clothing?
    - A. Long pants (as opposed to knee-length pants)
    - B. A tie (as opposed to a cravat)
    - C. A powdered wig

53. What state was James Madison from?
    - A. Wisconsin
    - B. North Carolina
    - C. Virginia

54. True or False? Madison was a champion of the Bill of Rights?

55. True or False? Madison was the last President elected who signed the Declaration of Independence?

56. What political party did Madison belong to?
     A. Federalist
     B. Democratic-Republican
     C. Whig

57. Madison had a reputation for being...?
     A. Stubborn
     B. Cheerful
     C. Talkative

58. True or False? Dolley Madison was the first First Lady to fully embrace the role of hostess and was a charismatic and popular woman?

59. True or False? When Washington D.C. was on the verge of being sacked in the War of 1812, Dolley Madison rescued some important papers and a painting of George Washington just before she fled to safety?

TEXT OF THE CONSTITUTION

60. What part of the United States Constitution includes the following text?

We the people of the United States, in order to form a more perfect union, establish justice, insure domestic tranquility, provide for the common defense, promote the general welfare, and secure the blessings of liberty to ourselves and our posterity, do ordain and establish this Constitution for the United States of America.

     A.   Preamble
     B.   Article I
     C.   Article IX

61. According to the text of the U.S. Constitution, how long is the term of a United States Senator?
     A.   2 years
     B.   4 years
     C.   6 years

62. In case of a tie, who casts the deciding vote in the U.S. Senate?
     A.   Sergeant-at-arms
     B.   Speaker Pro Tempore
     C.   Vice President

63. The starting number of Representatives to the House of Representatives is included in the Constitution. Which state began with the most?
    A. New York
    B. Pennsylvania
    C. Virginia

64. You have to be at least how old to be president of the United States?
    A. 30
    B. 35
    C. 40

65. Among the more controversial and less savory aspects of the (unamended) Constitution is that slaves are only counted as a fraction of a free person for the purposes of determining the number of representatives in Congress. According to the Constitution what fraction should slaves be counted as?
    A. Two fifths
    B. Three fifths
    C. Four fifths

66. According to the Constitution, how often is Congress required to meet?
    A. Once a year
    B. Twice a year
    C. There is no meeting requirement in the Constitution

67. When was the most recent special session of Congress?
    A. 1948
    B. 1986
    C. 2011

68. True or False. In the event that the House of Representatives and the Senate cannot agree on when Congress should adjourn, the president can order Congress to adjourn?

69. True or False. The Constitution successfully addressed many of the economic issues with the Articles of Confederation?

70. True or False. Although not perfect, the Constitution has been successful at preventing the return of the government tyranny that sparked the War of Independence?

71. The power of the federal government to review the Constitutionality of laws was another extensively debated topic. Some thought that Congress should be able to review and strike down invalid state laws. Where is the power to review laws to determine whether they are constitutional located in Constitution?
     A. Article I (Legislative Branch)
     B. Article II (Executive Branch)
     C. Article III (Judicial Branch)
     D. None of the above

72. Which of the following is a function that the Constitution prefers that the federal government handle?
     A. Commerce
     B. Education

73. Which of the following is a function that the Constitution prefers that state governments handle?
     A. Commerce
     B. Education

BILL OF RIGHTS

74. The first ten amendments are known as the Bill of Rights. Match the number of the amendment to the correct letter. For example, if you think that A describes the 8th amendment you would write an 8 in front of the A.

The right...

    A. To a jury trial in a civil suit where the amount in controversy exceeds $20

    B. To petition government for the redress of grievances

    C. To prevent the quartering of soldiers in a house except as prescribed by law

    D. To not be charged excessive bail

    E. To confront witnesses against you in a criminal trial

    F. To be free from unreasonable searches and seizures

    G. That all other rights not listed are retained by the people and the states

    H. That the enumeration of certain rights does not preclude other rights

    I. To keep and bear arms

    J. To no loss of liberty without due process of law

75. What year was the Bill of Rights ratified?
      A. 1792
      B. 1796
      C. 1800

76. Which of the following best describes the national government created by the Constitution and the Bill of Rights?
      A. A national government of almost unlimited power
      B. A national government of very limited power

ANSWERS

CONSTITUTIONAL CONVENTION

1. A. The original purpose of the Philadelphia Conference of 1787 was to discuss amending the Articles of Confederation. Later this meeting became known as the Constitutional Convention because the discussion moved almost immediately to the subject of creating a new constitution. Some of the delegates were eager to create a new constitution; others were more reluctant.

2. A. Although the concept had been discussed for years, the Articles of Confederation were formally proposed in 1776 during the Revolutionary War. On November 15, 1777, the Continental Congress approved the Articles of Confederation. It was then up to the states to ratify the Articles.

3. A. All of the states had ratified the Articles by March 1, 1781. Maryland was the last state to ratify them.

4. B. John Dickinson was the primary author of the Articles of Confederation. Dickinson was a lawyer and popular politician. Earlier he had helped draft the "Olive Branch" petition for the Continental Congress. He favored reconciliation rather than independence. In addition to the Continental Congress, he also served in elected office in both Pennsylvania and Delaware. He served as a delegate to the Convention from Delaware. He was one of the wealthiest men in America in his day. Later in life he favored abolition.

5. A. Zero. There are no presidents in the Articles of Confederation.

6. C. The Articles did not have a judicial branch at all. It had a very limited executive branch. The legislative branch was the strongest under the Articles.

7. True. The Articles had some definite weaknesses and these were seen as a threat to national unity. Many of the weaknesses of the Articles centered around economic issues such as currency and how trade between states should be regulated. The Articles left these issues up to the states. The trouble with economic issues

highlighted that it was very difficult to amend the Articles, a unanimous vote was required (each state got one vote) and 9 out of 13 states were required to approve national legislation. The inability to solve pressing trade and economic issues threatened national unity.

8. C. The Articles of Confederation protected states' rights. The Articles can be viewed as creating a league of friendship between the states. Cooperation was required. The central government was very weak, lacking the power of taxation. States had to voluntarily contribute money and no state ever gave the full amount asked of it.

9. B. Thomas Jefferson was abroad serving as the American ambassador to France. Given Jefferson's dynamic genius, it is very possible that the Constitution would have turned out differently if he had been one of the delegates to the Constitutional Convention. (Francis Marion was not a delegate. He was known for his guerrilla war prowess.)

10. B. Although they did not have the furthest to travel, perhaps ambivalent about the Convention, the New Hampshire delegation did not arrive until after the Convention had

already started. Delegates from other states were also late to the Convention.

11. B. George Washington presided over the Convention and served as an excellent moderator to the debates. He was no doubt helped in his job by the fact that he was held in high regard by all the delegates.

12. C. The Virginia plan proposed three co-presidents. The goal was to avoid tyranny. The number of presidents was one of the contentious issues at the convention.

13. A. Ben Franklin proposed the two-thirds requirement for veto overrides.

14. C. Charles Pinckney of South Carolina had many ideas similar to Madison that ultimately ended up in the Constitution. Years later Pinckney and Madison both shaded their own accounts of events. Pinckney had a greater reputation for exaggeration than Madison which complicates things. It is probably fair to consider Pinckney to be a "contributing writer" if not a co-author of the Constitution.

15. B. The New Jersey plan was concerned with how many Senators each state would

receive and whether the legislature would be unicameral or bicameral. The New Jersey plan was concerned with protecting the political power of smaller states.

16. B. For whatever reason the New York delegation could not get along and lost votes. Some states, such as Pennsylvania, had deliberately sent delegations of like-minded individuals and so had fewer intra-delegation disputes.

17. B. As was the custom of the Continental Congress, the states generally voted in order from north to south with New Hampshire voting first.

18. B. Roger Sherman helped broker compromises on the issues of how many senators each state received (the Connecticut Compromise), the three-fifths compromise (slavery), and executive powers. Each of these disputes had jeopardized the Convention. Sherman was the second oldest member of the Convention at 66 years old. Only Benjamin Franklin (81) was older.

19. A. Gouverneur Morris of Pennsylvania is the correct answer. If Madison was the primary author of the Constitution, Morris

was the editor. Gouvernor Morris was a proponent of a stronger national government spoke frequently during the Convention (only James Madison spoke more often).

20. B. The Continental Congress had met in many locations including Philadelphia, Trenton, Princeton, Lancaster, York, and Annapolis. At the time of the Convention it was meeting in New York City. Later, when George Washington was president, New York City was the capitol of the United States. The Constitution does include a clause about creating a capitol but that city was not ready at the time that Washington was president.

21. C. Rhode Island sent no delegates to the Convention.

22. B. Rhode Island was one of the few states that was happy with the status quo under the Articles of Confederation. It saw no need to amend or replace the Articles.

23. C. As a result of being slow to ratify the Constitution, Rhode Island was ineligible to participate in the first presidential election, held in 1789.

24. B. No. There was not an extensive public record of the Convention. The meetings were closed to the public and to the press. Very few notes were taken of the meeting. James Madison kept the most extensive notes. These notes were not published until many years later.

25. B. The Convention met from May 25 to September 17, 1787. It was supposed to start earlier in May but as noted in a previous question, delegates from many states were late to arrive and a quorum was not present until May 25.

RATIFICATION

26. C. There was no deadline for ratifying the Constitution. It only took effect if enough states ratified it (9 out of 13). It would only be in force in the states that ratified it.

27. A. Generally, state ratifying conventions lasted about a week. In the larger states, the conventions typically lasted about a month. It often took the states much longer to hold elections to determine delegates to the state conventions than it took the assembled delegates to debate and vote on the Constitution.

28. B. The Federalist Papers were an anonymous series of editorials that were written in support of the Constitution. The editorials were signed with the pen-name of Publius. The editorials were widely published in newspapers, particularly in New York City. They provide a window into how some of the founders thought that the Constitution would or should work. There are 85 separate essays in the Federalist Papers and the first one appeared in print on October 27, 1787.

29. C. Alexander Hamilton wrote the most Federalist Papers.

30. A. John Jay wrote only a few of the Federalist Papers. Jay later was appointed the first Chief Justice of the United States Supreme Court.

31. A. Delaware was the first state to ratify the Constitution (December 7, 1787). As was true for the other early states, the ratification in Delaware was unanimous.

32. A. New Hampshire was the ninth and deciding state to ratify the Constitution (June 21, 1788). Virginia ratified the Constitution four days later (June 25, 1788).

33. B. Rhode Island was the last state to ratify. It reluctantly did so on May 29, 1790. The vote was close. 34 in favor of ratification and 32 opposed. Rhode Island was persuaded in part by the United States Congress passing economic sanctions that made it illegal to trade with Rhode Island. The sanctions were lifted once Rhode Island ratified the Constitution. Rhode Island was opposed to ratification because it preferred to print its own money and because it did not like the way slavery was treated by the Constitution. Rhode Island favored the immediate abolition of slavery. For its resistance to ratification it was nicknamed "rogue island". Fun little bit of presidential election trivia: the question refers to the Presidential Election of 1789. The voting for the first election began in December of 1788 and did not conclude until January of 1789; it was not until the next cycle (1792) that elections were held in the fall.

34. C. Generally speaking, opponents of the ratification were referred to as antifederalists.

35. B. Three states, New Hampshire, North Carolina and Rhode Island, did not ratify on the first attempt.

36. C. Four states had adopted the Constitution by January 3, 1788. Those four states were Delaware, Pennsylvania, New Jersey, and Georgia.

37. B. The debate in Connecticut was harmonious. Those who opposed the Constitution did not leave the debate mad when the vote went against them 128 to 40. Connecticut was the fifth state to ratify (January 9, 1788).

38. A. The vote in Georgia was unanimous (26 to 0) in favor of ratification and the Constitution was debated for only one day. Georgia was the fourth state to ratify (January 2, 1788).

39. B. The New Jersey ratification convention took place at the Blazing Star tavern. The vote was unanimous (38 to 0) in favor of ratification. New Jersey was the third state to ratify (December 18, 1787).

40. C. The New York Convention was held in Poughkeepsie. Poughkeepsie is along the Hudson river about halfway between Albany and New York City. Since New York would be the eleventh state to ratify, much of the debate centered on what

amendments New York would recommend to the First Congress (July 26, 1788).

41. B. In the summer of 1788, the North Carolina Convention met in Hillsborough at St. Matthews Church. After 12 days they voted to reject the Constitution by a vote of 184 to 83. After a Bill of Rights was proposed in Congress, North Carolina ratified the Constitution on November 21, 1789. Like Rhode Island, North Carolina missed out on participating in the Presidential Election of 1789 because it had not ratified the Constitution in time.

42. C. In South Carolina, the Constitution was ratified by a vote of 149 to 73. Ratification was aided by the fact that the interior of the state, which was generally opposed to the Constitution, was underrepresented at the state convention. The South Carolina Convention also passed some amendments for the First Congress to consider. Despite underrepresentation, the convention process worked in South Carolina. Both sides were happy with the convention and there was no unhappy dissent, unlike in some other states. South Carolina was the eighth state to ratify (May 23, 1788).

43. A. George Washington sent a letter to one of his former officers, Benjamin Lincoln of Massachusetts, in support of ratification, knowing that the letter would be shared with others. George Washington kept track of the news of the state conventions from his Mount Vernon estate. Most people expected that George Washington would be elected the first president of the United States once the Constitution was ratified.

44. True. If the Constitution was not ratified in Massachusetts, probably New York and New Hampshire would follow in rejecting it. A negative outcome in those states would make Virginia less likely to ratify. At the time of the Massachusetts Convention Rhode Island showed no interest in ratification. If those all those states failed to ratify that would defeat ratification because 9 out of 13 states had to ratify. The vote in Massachusetts was 187 to 168. Although state conventions were only allowed to vote to accept or reject the Constitution, Massachusetts began the practice of accepting the Constitution and recommending amendments for the First Congress to consider. Massachusetts was the sixth state to ratify and almost all of the states that ratified after Massachusetts proposed amendments (February 6, 1788).

45. True. The convention process did not work well in Pennsylvania. The Pennsylvania Convention was long and drawn out over several weeks and had so many federalist delegates that the outcome was never in doubt. The final vote was 2 to 1 in favor of ratification. The bad feelings generated by the Pennsylvania Convention spilled over into neighboring states. Pennsylvania was the second state to ratify (December 12, 1788).

46. C. In Maryland there was a large majority for ratification (the vote was 63-11). Many delegates wanted amendments but none were officially recommended by the Maryland Convention. The disappointed delegates complained bitterly. Maryland was the seventh state to ratify (April 28, 1788).

47. A. The biggest and most common objections to the Constitution were that it lacked a Bill of Rights. Congressional taxing powers were also a common concern. Slavery was another big issue that was raised in many debates.

48. A. New Hampshire was the first state to fail to ratify the Constitution at a state

convention. New Hampshire voted to adjourn after 9 days without passing the Constitution. It was a safety move by the federalists to avoid the failure of rejection. The motion to adjourn barely passed 65 to 61. New Hampshire adjourned from February until June. New Hampshire would be the ninth and deciding state to ratify, ratifying four days before Virginia in July of 1788.

49. B. On September 13, 1788, almost a year after the Constitutional Convention had adjourned, Congress officially certified that the Constitution had been ratified and set the dates for the first election under the new Constitution.

JAMES MADISON

50. C. James Madison is most famous for his considerable involvement with the drafting and design of the Constitution.

51. A. Madison was one of the shortest presidents. He was only 5'4" tall.

52. A. James Madison was the first president to wear long pants (as opposed to knee-length pants).

53. C. James Madison was from Virginia. The state capitol of Wisconsin is named in his honor.

54. True. Madison was a champion of the Bill of Rights.

55. True. Madison was the last President elected who signed the Declaration of Independence.

56. B. Madison belonged to the Democratic-Republican party. This party became the modern Democratic party.

57. A. Madison had a reputation for being stubborn.

58. True. Dolley Madison was the first First Lady to fully embrace the role of hostess and was a charismatic and popular woman.

59. True. When Washington D.C. was on the verge of being sacked in the War of 1812, Dolley Madison rescued some important papers and a painting of George Washington just before she fled to safety.

TEXT OF THE CONSTITUTION

60. A. The words "We the people of the United States, in order to form a more perfect union, establish justice, insure domestic tranquility, provide for the common defense, promote the general welfare, and secure the blessings of liberty to ourselves and our posterity, do ordain and establish this Constitution for the United States of America" are from the Preamble.

61. C. According to the Constitution, United States Senators are elected to terms of 6 years.

62. C. The vice president casts the tie-breaking vote in the Senate.

63. C. Virginia had ten representatives. The next highest state was Pennsylvania with eight. New York had six then; now it has 29. The national census that occurs every ten years determines the number of representatives for each state for the coming decade.

64. B. You have to be at least 35 years old to be elected president of the United States.

65. B. As a compromise in the drafting of the Constitution, slaves were to be counted as

three-fifths of a person for the purposes of determining the number of representatives a state received in Congress. The three-fifths clause was effectively abolished when the Thirteenth Amendment outlawed slavery in the United States.

66. A. It is mandatory that Congress meet at least once a year.

67. A. Coming out of an English heritage where kings tended to abuse Parliament, the Constitution has much greater limitations on the president's ability to control when Congress meets. The president has a discretionary power to convene Congress in extraordinary situations. The special session power has been used 27 times. As Congress is generally in session year round now, with short recesses, the last special session was called by President Truman on July 15, 1948, prior to that a special session had not been called since 1856.

68. True. The House and the Senate must agree on when to adjourn and if they do not agree, the president can act as tie-breaker by ordering them to adjourn or stay in session. This is the only presidential power that has never been used.

69. True. The Constitution has worked well to address the shortcomings of the Articles of Confederation. The Constitution gave the federal government greater control over key economic issues such as currency and regulating trade.

70. True. Although not perfect, through a system of checks and balances the Constitution has worked to prevent the return of government tyranny that was the cause of the War of Independence.

71. D. The express power of reviewing laws for their constitutionality is not in the Constitution. Generally that power has been located in the judicial branch following the 1803 decision of *Marbury v. Madison*.

72. A. Commerce is regulated more by the federal government than the states. States are still allowed to regulate commerce. However, they can be overruled by what Congress decides in the matter. Wealthy delegates often favored the commerce benefits offered by the Constitution.

73. B. Education is generally left up to the states by the Constitution. Since the 1950s, the federal government has taken a greater role in education.

BILL OF RIGHTS

74. Matching Answers:

A. The 7th Amendment provides for the right to a jury trial in civil suits.

B. Petition the government is a 1st Amendment right.

C. Limitations on quartering of soldiers are found in the 3rd Amendment.

D. No excessive bail is in the 8th Amendment.

E. The right to confront witnesses is part of the 6th Amendment.

F. Search and seizure is restricted by the 4th Amendment.

G. All other rights retained by the people and the states in the 10th Amendment.

H. The enumeration of certain rights does not preclude other rights is found in the 9th Amendment.

I. The 2nd Amendment has the right to bear arms.

J. The 5th Amendment protects against loss of liberty without due process.

75. A. The Bill of Rights was formally ratified on March 1, 1792. The rights had been submitted to the states in a group of 12 but only 10 rights were passed by a sufficient number of states. An amendment regarding direct taxation and the future 27th Amendment concerning restrictions on laws

affecting changes in Congressional pay were not ratified.

76. B. The Constitution and the Bill of Rights create a national government of very limited power. Most of the power is held by the states and the people.

SCORING

Generally more than 50% correct is a good score.

Regardless of how many you got correct, I hope these questions were fun and prompt you to learn more about the U.S Constitution!

BIBLIOGRAPHY AND SUGGESTED RESOURCES

Agel, Jerome and Gerberg, Mort. *The U.S. Declaration of Independence for everyone*. New York : Penguin Putnam, Inc., 2001.

Beeman, Richard. *Plain, honest men : the making of the American Constitution*. New York : Random House, 2009.

Brennan, Stephen. *The U.S. Constitution and related documents*. New York : Skyhorse Publishing, 2011.

Carey, George W., and McClellan, James. *The Federalist : The Gideon Edition*. Indianapolis : Liberty Fund, 2001.

De Bolla, Peter. *The Fourth of July and the Founding of America*. New York : Overlook Press, 2007.

Ellis, Joseph J. *Revolutionary summer : the birth of American independence.* New York : Alfred A. Knopf, 2013.

January, Brendan. *James Madison*. New York : Children's Press, 2003.

Maier, Pauline. *Ratification: The people debate the Constitution 1787-1788*. New York : Simon & Schuster, 2010.

McCullough, David. *1776.* New York : Simon and Schuster, 2007.

Meese, Edwin and Spalding, Mathew, and Forte, David. *The Heritage Guide to the Constitution*. Washington D.C. : Regnery Publishing, Inc., 2005.

Middlekauff, Robert. *The Glorious Cause : The American Revolution, 1763-1789*. New York : Oxford University Press, 2005.

Rodell, Fred. *55 Men The story of the Constitution : Based on the day-by-day notes of James Madison*. Harrisburg, PA : Stackpole Books, 1986.

Sonneborn, Liz. *The Articles of Confederation*. Chicago : Heinemann Library, 2013.

http://www.politico.com/news/stories/0707/5104.html

ABOUT THE AUTHOR

The author is a lawyer who lives with his family near St. Paul, Minnesota. Some of the other quiz books he has written include: *Santa Claus's Christmas Trivia Challenge: 100 questions about the secular and sacred customs of Christmas*, *Easter Trivia Challenge* and *George Washington's Monumental Presidential Trivia Challenge : More than 500 questions about the 44 U.S. Presidents from Washington to Obama*.

www.ingramcontent.com/pod-product-compliance
Lightning Source LLC
Chambersburg PA
CBHW071641170526
45166CB00003B/1389